SCHOLASTIC

ACTIVE English Workbook 8

Name: ______________________________

Class: ______________________________

Scholastic India Pvt. Ltd.
A-27, Ground Floor, Bharti Sigma Centre
Infocity-1, Sector 34, Gurgaon (Haryana) 122001, India
Email: info_in@scholastic.asia

Rest of the World
Scholastic Education International (Singapore) Pte Ltd
81 Ubi Avenue 4 #02-28 UB.ONE Singapore 408830
Email: education_sg@scholastic.asia

Visit our website: www.scholastic.co.in

First edition: 2012
Reprinted: 2012, 2014 (twice), 2015, 2016, 2017, 2019, 2020

ISBN-978-81-8477-739-0

Preface

The creators of ACTIVE™ **English** believe that literacy acquisition is dependent on the integrated teaching of reading, writing, listening and speaking skills, and the engagement of learners. This integrated approach to learning and literacy development is advocated through a systematic and consistent instructional design and scope and sequence.

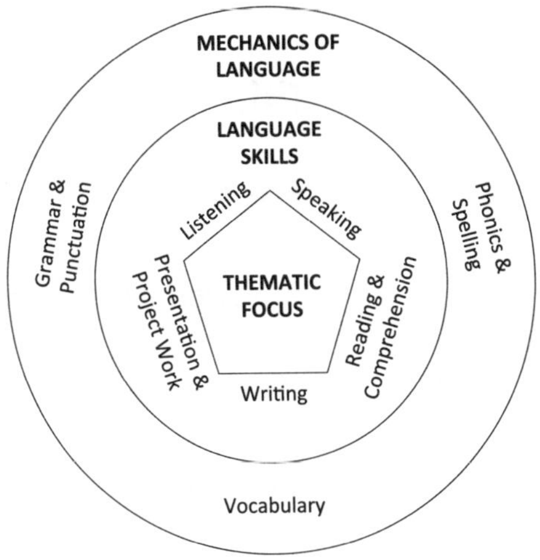

This Workbook can be used to extend the learning in the Coursebook or as an independent learning resource.

Coursebook Correlation to Extend Learning

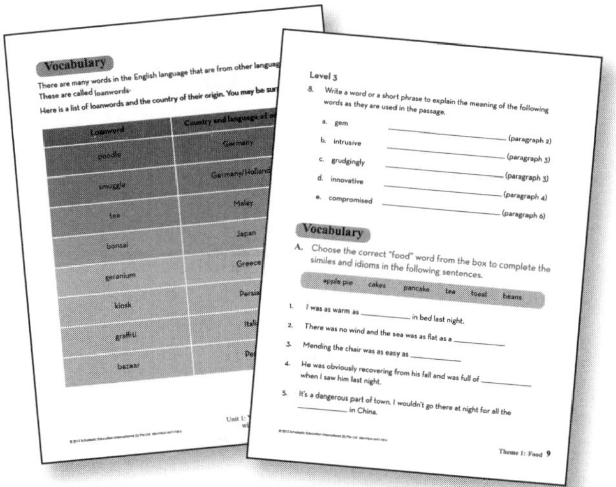

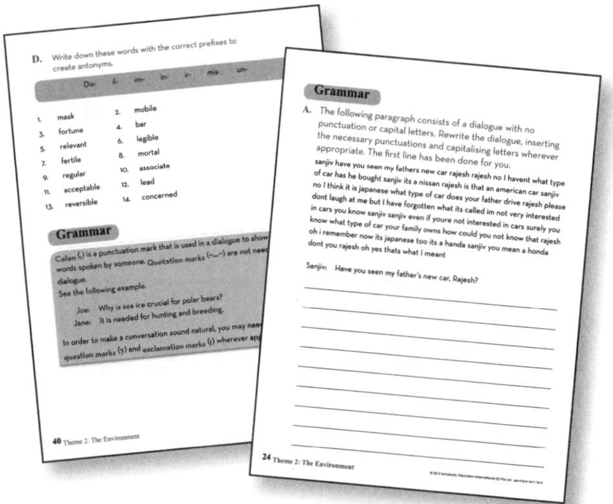

Each theme in the Workbook correlates to a theme in the Coursebook in terms of its topic and language skills. The exercises provide additional practice for reinforcement and consolidation.

Authentic and Varied Text Types

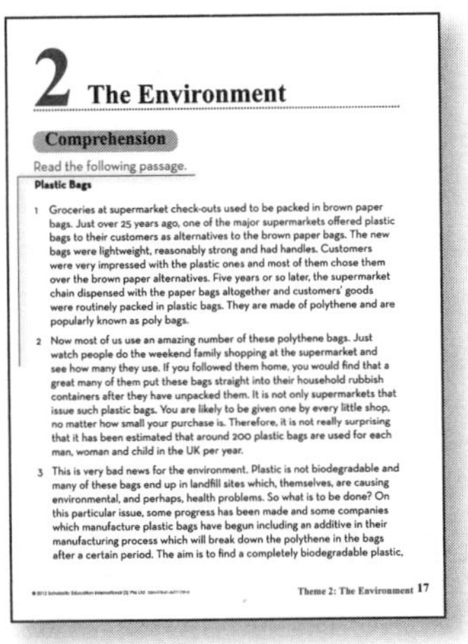

Authentic texts in a variety of text types engage students and prepare them for language in the real world.

Integration of Language Skills

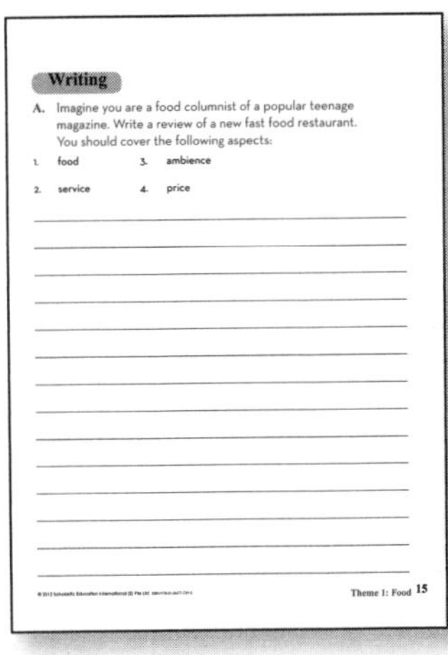

The writing exercises in each unit consolidate the language skills covered in the Coursebook and provide extension activities for the comprehension passage.

Contents

 ISBN-978-81-8477-739-0

1 Food

Comprehension

Read the following restaurant review.

A Vegetarian's Answer to Good Food

1 Vegetarians tend to have a hard time when they travel. The situation is better in the UK than in most of Europe, but that's not saying much. Usually, vegetarians have little choice but to make for the nearest pizza place or to settle for salad and chips or a soggy vegetable lasagne at the local pub.

2 What a delight it was, then, to come across Country Life in the little town of Longchurch. It is an absolute gem of a place, right on the high street. When we ate there, our only regret was that we were only staying one night in Longchurch and so could only eat there once. We wanted to bring it home with us!

3 The restaurant is situated in a pretty yellow and blue room with comfortable pine furniture and pictures by local artists on the walls, a change from the minimalist décor that we city-eaters have had to get used to recently. The service was excellent – attentive but not at all intrusive. We had hardly sat down at the smart gingham-covered tables when a plate of the most delicious brown bread I have ever tasted was put on the table, accompanied by a jug of ice-cold water and four glasses. What a refreshing change! Usually you have to ask for tap water and it is often given grudgingly by a restaurateur who would rather charge you for bottled water!

4 The food was innovative, even eclectic, but the flavours all combined together wonderfully well, which is not always the case with inventive food. Starters included two delicious soups – a sweetcorn soup with red pepper puree and a pumpkin and ginger soup. On the starter menu also were a warm courgette salad and a vegetarian leek sausage, flavoured with rosemary and thyme, and served with cranberry sauce.

 ISBN-978-81-8477-739-0

5 Main courses included creamy onion crepes; yellow peppers stuffed with pistachios and smoked tofu soufflé served with an orange sauce, and leek and tofu pie served with an onion sauce. Alternatively, you could have an aubergine and cashew nut roulade served with a sweet and sour sauce; spinach parcels filled with black-eyed peas and served with pine nut cakes; or char-grilled vegetables served with salsa. It took us ages to make our choice! The main courses were accompanied by a selection of steamed vegetables cooked just right, neither cooked to a pulp, nor still brick-hard.

6 After all this, we did not really have room for dessert, but we simply could not resist them. We compromised by sharing two among four. We had a delicious lemon tart, topped with red currants, and an equally delicious orange sponge cake, topped with raspberries and served with some wonderful home-made vanilla ice cream. (Vegans will be pleased to know that they can have the orange cake, as it is made with corn oil and contains no eggs or dairy products; alas, this is not true of the ice cream). We could also have had gooseberry pie or a selection of cheeses but, as it was, we were absolutely full.

7 Visiting the Country Life was altogether a delightful experience and I am now seeking an excuse to go back to Longchurch. We live 200 miles away and that is a little far to drive for dinner!

Tel: 0251 556 6342
Open for dinner only: 6 pm until 10.30 pm
Closed Sundays and Christmas Day
No smoking
Car park
Wheelchair access
All major credit cards accepted

 ISBN-978-81-8477-739-0

A. Answer the following questions.

Level 1

1. In what style are most restaurants decorated nowadays?

____

____

2. How many choices of starters were there at the restaurant in Longchurch?

____

____

3. What was the standard serving that came with every main dish?

____

____

4. What factor made it difficult for the writer to patronise Country Life regularly?

____

____

Level 2

5. What complaint does the writer make on behalf of all vegetarians concerning food?

____

____

 ISBN-978-81-8477-739-0

6. Briefly describe the difference in customer service in a regular restaurant and Country Life.

____

____

7. Based on the gastronomic fare described by the writer, draw up a shopping list for the restaurant along the broad categories given below. The first item has been done to help you.

Shopping list					
Vegetables	Fruit	Nuts	Herbs	Bottled sauces	Miscellaneous food
sweet corn					

 ISBN-978-81-8477-739-0

Level 3

8. Write a word or a short phrase to explain the meaning of the following words as they are used in the passage.

   a. gem ______________________ (paragraph 2)

   b. intrusive ______________________ (paragraph 3)

   c. grudgingly ______________________ (paragraph 3)

   d. innovative ______________________ (paragraph 4)

   e. compromised ______________________ (paragraph 6)

Vocabulary

A. Choose the correct "food" word from the box to complete the similes and idioms in the following sentences.

apple pie	cakes	pancake	tea	toast	beans

1. I was as warm as ____________ in bed last night.
2. There was no wind and the sea was as flat as a ____________.
3. Mending the chair was as easy as ____________.
4. He was obviously recovering from his fall and was full of ____________ when I saw him last night.
5. It's a dangerous part of town. I wouldn't go there at night for all the ____________ in China.

 ISBN-978-81-8477-739-0

B. Decide which set of ingredients corresponds to which item of food in the box.

curry	cake	ice cream	soup	omelette	pizza

1. strawberries, cream, sugar ____________
2. flour, yeast, salt, olive oil, cheese, tomatoes, ham ____________
3. flour, butter, sugar, eggs, milk, baking powder, chocolate powder ____________
4. eggs, cheese, herbs ____________
5. oil, onions, chillies, garlic, yogurt, tomatoes, coconut, peppers, spices ____________
6. tomatoes, olive oil, onions, carrots, celery, salt, pepper, sugar, cream ____________

C. A list of phrases that describes problems is given below. Some phrases describe small problems, others more serious problems. Put the phrases into three groups according to how serious the problem seems to be.

a slight difficulty	a major obstacle	an insurmountable problem
a slight hitch	a minor setback	quite a challenge
an absolute disaster	a bit of a puzzle	a big problem
a slight complication	a spot of bother	rather a dilemma
quite a predicament	a bit of a jam	a snag
a catastrophe		

 ISBN-978-81-8477-739-0

Small problems	Serious problems	Very serious problems

Grammar

A. In each of the following sentences, fill in the blank with the imperative form of the verb which is underlined elsewhere in the sentence.

1. The notice on the door read "Please ____________ the bell," so we <u>rang</u> the bell and waited for someone to come.

2. You should have <u>told</u> him that last night. Go and ____________ him now.

3. The floor hasn't been <u>swept</u> since last week. Please ____________ it this morning.

 ISBN-978-81-8477-739-0

4. "________________!" I shouted, and we both <u>ran</u> as fast as we could.

5. She didn't understand what you <u>said</u>. ________________ it again more slowly.

6. "Please ________________ down," he said, pointing to the chair. So I <u>sat</u> down and watched him.

7. The recipe said, "________________ the chocolate into small pieces," so I <u>broke</u> it up with a large wooden spoon.

8. "Please ________________ me," she said, with tears in her eyes. So of course I <u>forgave</u> her at once.

B. Fill in the blanks in the following paragraph with verbs in the future continuous tense, using the words provided in the box.

shine	play	sunbathe	stay	sleep	build
have	swim	read	share	do	

This time next week I will be on holiday with my family. We ____________ in a big hotel beside the sea. My brother and I ____________ a room, but my little sister ____________ in the same room as our mother and father. I wonder what we ____________ while we are at the seaside. I imagine that in the mornings, we ____________ on the beach. I do hope the sun ____________! In the afternoons, my brother and I ____________ in the sea, or perhaps we ____________ football or cricket on the sand. Mum and Dad ____________ books. My little sister ____________ sandcastles. I'm sure we ____________ a lot of fun.

 ISBN-978-81-8477-739-0

C. Fill in the blanks in the following sentences with verbs in the past continuous tense, using the words provided in the box.

dig	laugh	ride	hope	cry	bark

1. Amanda ______________ her bike along the road when suddenly a dog ran out in front of her. It ______________ furiously.

2. He ______________ a hole in the garden to plant a tree when he came across a strange wooden box.

3. I don't know why Jane ______________ when she left the room, or why John ______________ at her.

4. We ______________ to see the Queen drive past but there were too many people in front of us.

D. In each of the following sentences, fill in the blank with the future tense form of the verb which is underlined elsewhere in the sentence.

1. I <u>saw</u> him yesterday and I'm sure I ____________________ him again today.

2. The price of milk <u>rose</u> by 3% last year. I expect it ____________________ even more this year.

3. I have <u>said</u> it before and I ____________________ it again: I don't trust him.

4. The old mast <u>snapped</u> during the storm but this one is stronger and I don't think it ____________________ even in a hurricane.

 ISBN-978-81-8477-739-0

5. I have already <u>sold</u> most of my chickens and I ______________ the rest of them at the market next week.

6. Most of the soldiers have already <u>left</u> and the rest ______________ by the end of the year.

7. It was so cold last night that the water <u>froze</u>. I wonder if it ______________ ______________ again tonight.

E. Future and continuous tenses of verbs can be separated into two parts by adverbs. In each of the following sentences, fill in each blank with one of the adverbs provided in the box.

Note: The last two sentences need two adverbs each. There can be more than one correct answer.

already	still	probably	just
never	desperately	possibly	simply

1. We were ______________ leaving the restaurant when it started to rain.
2. Smoke and flames were ______________ pouring out of the building by the time the fire engines appeared.
3. They were ______________ laughing when they left the theatre.
4. We were ______________ trying to avoid an argument.
5. We will ______________ be visiting them again next week.
6. I went to Egypt on holiday last year but I didn't like it, and I will ______________ go back there again.

 ISBN-978-81-8477-739-0

Writing

A. Imagine you are a food columnist of a popular teenage magazine. Write a review of a new fast food restaurant. You should cover the following aspects:

1. food
2. service
3. ambience
4. price

 ISBN-978-81-8477-739-0

B. Based on the review, *A Vegetarian's Answer to Good Food*, design the menu for Country Life. You will be assessed based on the appropriateness of style, presentation and content.

 ISBN-978-81-8477-739-0

2 The Environment

Comprehension

Read the following passage.

Plastic Bags

1 Groceries at supermarket check-outs used to be packed in brown paper bags. Just over 25 years ago, one of the major supermarkets offered plastic bags to their customers as alternatives to the brown paper bags. The new bags were lightweight, reasonably strong and had handles. Customers were very impressed with the plastic ones and most of them chose them over the brown paper alternatives. Five years or so later, the supermarket chain dispensed with the paper bags altogether and customers' goods were routinely packed in plastic bags. They are made of polythene and are popularly known as poly bags.

2 Now most of us use an amazing number of these polythene bags. Just watch people do the weekend family shopping at the supermarket and see how many they use. If you followed them home, you would find that a great many of them put these bags straight into their household rubbish containers after they have unpacked them. It is not only supermarkets that issue such plastic bags. You are likely to be given one by every little shop, no matter how small your purchase is. Therefore, it is not really surprising that it has been estimated that around 200 plastic bags are used for each man, woman and child in the UK per year.

3 This is very bad news for the environment. Plastic is not biodegradable and many of these bags end up in landfill sites which, themselves, are causing environmental, and perhaps, health problems. So what is to be done? On this particular issue, some progress has been made and some companies which manufacture plastic bags have begun including an additive in their manufacturing process which will break down the polythene in the bags after a certain period. The aim is to find a completely biodegradable plastic,

 ISBN-978-81-8477-739-0

but this, although an extremely welcome development, would not solve all the problems caused by the plastic bag.

4 There is the problem of litter. Plastic bags are easily blown about in wind and get themselves wrapped around lamp posts or stuck on trees, bushes and fences. To say the least, they are unsightly. However, it is not just their unsightliness that is the problem.

5 When dropped as litter, plastic bags can clog drains and prevent rainwater from escaping, thereby causing flood. This is particularly a problem in developing countries, where drainage systems are often not very efficient.

6 Plastic bags can present a danger to animals and birds. They swallow the plastic which can then get all tangled up in their stomachs. This is a particular hazard for grazing animals which come into contact with the litter of human beings. Thus, cows which wander the streets in some parts of India are particularly at risk, as are goats in the Middle East which investigate picnic litter left by tourists. Sea creatures are also at risk from plastic bags. The bags float about on the ocean and are consumed by whales, dolphins, porpoises et cetera.

7 Some countries are trying to discourage the use of plastic bags. Ireland has recently started charging 0.15 Euros for each bag. After a few months, it has been estimated that there has been a great decrease in the number of bags used. When faced with having to pay for something which they formerly got for nothing, customers are either reusing the bags which they obtained on previous shopping trips or are using other kinds of bags or containers to carry home their shopping.

8 Taiwan is also taking measures against the overuse of plastic bags. Currently, all shops on government premises, such as military bases or university campuses, have to impose a charge for the bags. This rule is shortly to be extended to all shops and stores and, later, to all market traders.

9 Other countries are watching the situation in Ireland and Taiwan with interest and are contemplating following suit. However, many of them are afraid that people will object strongly to paying for something which they regard as part of the shopping experience and which they have always had for free.

 ISBN-978-81-8477-739-0

10 Attempts to persuade people to recycle their plastic bags are not proving very successful. People who have a concern for the environment do save their plastic bags and use them again and again, but most people just throw them away and start again on the next lot. Some shops, other than supermarkets, have begun to ask customers if they would like their goods to be put in a bag, if they are not buying quite much, rather than putting the goods in a plastic bag automatically. Apparently, quite a few customers do refuse the bag, but such a saving of plastic bags is a drop in the ocean.

11 The overuse of plastic bags is a very serious problem and it is a global one. It is time that governments on a global scale got together to try and solve it.

A. Answer the following questions.

Level 1

1. What advantages do polythene bags have over paper ones?

____

____

2. What is the ultimate solution to the health and environmental problem of plastic bags accumulating in landfill sites?

____

____

3. State the action taken by Ireland and Taiwan to discourage the use of plastic bags.

____

____

 ISBN-978-81-8477-739-0

4. What have some shops and supermarkets begun to do to play their part in controlling the use of plastic bags?

Level 2

5. Describe the common behaviour of people when they use plastic bags.

6. How do plastic bags affect our physical environment?

7. What dangers does plastic bag litter pose to animals?

 ISBN-978-81-8477-739-0

8. In the table below, fill in the cause and effect relationship between plastic bags and the environment.

Cause	Effect
non-biodegradable plastic buried in landfill sites	
plastic thrown as litter in the open	
plastic thrown as litter into drains	
plastic thrown as litter into seas	

Level 3

9. Write a word or short phrase to explain the meaning of the following words as they are used in the passage.

a. check-outs ______________________________ (paragraph 1)

b. routinely ______________________________ (paragraph 1)

c. tangled ______________________________ (paragraph 6)

d. contemplating ______________________________ (paragraph 9)

e. a drop in the ocean ______________________________ (paragraph 10)

 ISBN-978-81-8477-739-0

Vocabulary

A. Circle the word that is not a synonym of the word in bold print.

1.	**harmful**	destructive	delicate	damaging	detrimental
2.	**main**	leading	minor	foremost	principal
3.	**intention**	aim	goal	purpose	connection
4.	**abundant**	negligible	plentiful	ample	copious
5.	**conclusion**	finding	verdict	deduction	assumption

B. Replace the words in bold print with antonyms from the box.

immense	weak	lower	serious	plentiful
gradual	beneficial	permanent		

1. a **harmful** effect ______________
2. a **trivial** problem ______________
3. a **temporary** solution ______________
4. a **minuscule** amount ______________
5. a **scarce** resource ______________
6. a **sudden** change ______________
7. a **strong** argument ______________
8. a **higher** priority ______________

 ISBN-978-81-8477-739-0

C. The following paragraph contains some words that have been misspelled. Underline and rewrite the word correctly in the space given below.

Are we seeing the begining of the end of life on Earth as we have known

____

it? Our planet may be the only one in the whole unniverse that can suport

____

human life, but our human activities are making this home of ours almost

____

imposible to live on. We all know that the Earth's ressources are not

____

unlimmited, but they are being exploited to such an extent that they might

____

never recover. We are seeing serius deforrestation – in some parts of the

____

world, tropikal rainforrests are being torn down in order to acomodate

____

farms, plantations and ranches – and dramatic declines in numbers of fish

____

and other species. Indeed, many animal and plant species have already

____

dissappeared. We could be heading for an imensse catastrophy.

____

 ISBN-978-81-8477-739-0

Grammar

A. The following paragraph consists of a dialogue with no punctuation or capital letters. Rewrite the dialogue, inserting the necessary punctuations and capitalising letters wherever appropriate. The first line has been done for you.

sanjiv have you seen my fathers new car rajesh rajesh no I havent what type of car has he bought sanjiv its a nissan rajesh is that an american car sanjiv no I think it is japanese what type of car does your father drive rajesh please dont laugh at me but I have forgotten what its called im not very interested in cars you know sanjiv sanjiv even if youre not interested in cars surely you know what type of car your family owns how could you not know that rajesh oh i remember now its japanese too its a handa sanjiv you mean a honda dont you rajesh oh yes thats what I meant

Sanjiv: Have you seen my father's new car, Rajesh?

 ISBN-978-81-8477-739-0

B. The following paragraph describes a conversation between two people. Rewrite this conversation as a dialogue. The first line has been done for you.

(Note: In writing the dialogue, you should ignore any part of the paragraph below that does not report the words that were said.)

The police officer stopped Tim and asked him where he was going. Tim replied that he was going to visit a friend. The officer asked Tim where his friend lived, to which Tim replied that he lived in Essex Square. His house was just next to the bank. The officer asked Tim if his parents knew that he was walking around town alone at that time of night, and Tim assured him that yes, they did, and that they didn't mind him being out late at night. The officer said that was all right, but he warned Tim to be careful to avoid dark streets. Tim said he would.

Police officer: Where are you going?

 ISBN-978-81-8477-739-0

C. Rewrite the following sentences using the modal verbs given in brackets and making any other necessary changes.

For example:

It is possible that he will arrive tomorrow. (may)

He may arrive tomorrow.

1. It is possible that he will not come at all. (might)

____

2. Are you able to help us next Saturday? (can)

____

3. Is it possible for a snake to swallow an elephant? (could)

____

4. I presume, you are my new assistant. (must)

____

5. Would you be able to come next week? (could)

____

6. They will definitely have arrived by now. (must)

____

7. It is possible that I won't have finished reading the book by the end of the week. (may)

____

 ISBN-978-81-8477-739-0

8. It is impossible for me to lend you as much money as that. (can)

____

Writing

A. Working in a group of three or four, design a poster for your school to encourage your schoolmates to use fewer plastic bags. Keep in mind the following points while composing the poster.

1. Include what problems plastic bags will cause, drawing on the information from the passage *Plastic Bags*.

2. Use the Internet with your teacher's guidance to obtain statistics or other relevant information on the use of plastic bags in your country.

3. Include photos and illustrations, wherever appropriate.

B. Do a research on a group that fights for the cause of our environment. Write an informational text on:

1. who they are
2. their mission
3. their work
4. their accomplishments

____

____

____

____

____

 ISBN-978-81-8477-739-0

 ISBN-978-81-8477-739-0

3 Cautionary Tales

Comprehension

Read the following article from a reference book.

Chernobyl

1 Chernobyl, a town in the Ukraine (formerly part of the USSR), about 100 km north of Kiev, is the site of the world's largest-known nuclear disaster. The disaster took place on 26 April 1986 when the number 4 reactor in the nuclear power station near Chernobyl blew up, causing around 250 deaths and evacuation of 1,35,000 people from a 35-km zone around the town.

2 The nuclear accident was caused by an authorised experiment which went wrong. During the experiment, the reactor core was blown apart, releasing a large amount of radioactive material into the environment. It has been estimated that it was approximately equivalent to the fallout from the explosion of a very large atmospheric atomic bomb. Levels of radioactivity were found to be increased in many parts of the world, particularly northern and eastern Europe. Considerable quantities of agricultural produce had to be destroyed as they were unfit for human use and it was thought that grazing for sheep and cattle would be affected for a very long time after the event.

3 The problem, generally, was not just an immediate one, but the scale of the aftermath of the disaster was difficult to predict. It was feared that there would be a considerable rise in deaths from cancer and a rise in the number of deformed children born. The fire in the reactor and the escape of radioactive materials were ended by burying the reactor in concrete, but the fear associated with the event was not so easily suppressed.

 ISBN-978-81-8477-739-0

4 The Chernobyl disaster caused a great deal of unrest about nuclear reactors generally. It was argued in western countries that the design of nuclear reactors there was much safer and that operations were much more strictly controlled. However, many people remained unconvinced and the Chernobyl disaster led to a cancellation or cutting back of some nuclear energy programmes in the West.

A. Answer the following questions.

Level 1

1. What will history always remember Chernobyl for?

____

____

2. What is the predicted health hazard resulting from the disaster?

____

____

3. How was the dangerous situation finally managed?

____

____

4. What was the impact of Chernobyl on nuclear energy programmes in general?

____

____

 ISBN-978-81-8477-739-0

Level 2

5. How do we know that the fallout was literally far-reaching?

____

____

6. What answer did western countries give to people fearful about nuclear energy programmes?

____

____

7. The consequences of the Chernobyl nuclear disaster were immediate, short term and long term. Categorise these consequences in the given table below.

Consequences		
Immediate	Short term	Long term

Level 3

8. Write a word or a short phrase to explain the meaning of the following words as they are used in the passage.

   a. evacuation ______________________ (paragraph 1)

   b. authorised ______________________ (paragraph 2)

   c. considerable ______________________ (paragraph 2)

   d. suppressed ______________________ (paragraph 3)

Vocabulary

A. Pick out the examples of alliteration in the following verse of poetry and write down the words that alliterate.

I felt weary of wandering, and went down to rest
On a broad sheltered bank by a babbling **beck**,
And as I lay and leaned over and listened and looked,
I slumbered and slept, so sweet sounded the brook.

____

____

____

____

____

---

beck: small river

 ISBN-978-81-8477-739-0

B. Here is another verse of poetry. Pick out and write down three phrases that show assonance.

Hear the mellow wedding bells –
Golden bells!
What a world of happiness their harmony foretells!
Through the balmy air of night
How they ring out their delight!
From the molten-golden notes,
And all in tune,
What a liquid ditty floats
To the turtle-dove that listens, while she gloats
On the moon!

 ISBN-978-81-8477-739-0

C. Match the countries with the units of currency listed below. Write in the space provided.

China	France	United Kingdom
Mexico	Bangladesh	South Africa

1. Euro ______________
2. Yuan ______________
3. Pound ______________
4. Peso ______________
5. Taka ______________
6. Rand ______________

D. Fill in the blanks in the following dialogue using the words provided in the box.

dividend	investment	shareholder	profits	prices	ownership
certificate	exchanges	document	stocks	worth	

Shaheed: Can you tell me something about stocks and shares, Salman?

Salman: "______________" and "shares" are the same thing. If you own shares in a company, you are a ______________. That means you have a share in the ______________ of that company. The shares you own are represented by a share ______________, which is a ______________ that proves you own the shares. The more shares you own, the larger the share of the company's ______________ you get. The money

 ISBN-978-81-8477-739-0

shareholders receive from a company is called a ______________. Shareholders also hope that the shares will one day be ______________ more than the price they paid for them. Shareholders can earn a lot of money if a company is successful, but they may lose their ______________ if the company isn't successful. People buy and sell shares in stock ______________, which exist in just about every country in the world. Share ______________ change every day.

Grammar

A. In the following pairs of sentences, fill in the blank in the second sentence with a compound word that means the same as the underlined words in the first sentence. All the compound words are hyphenated.

1. The stones were <u>covered in moss</u>.
   He slipped on the ______________ stones.

2. All the cakes had been <u>made at home</u>.
   All the cakes were ______________.

3. The mountains had <u>caps of snow</u>.
   We looked out at the ______________ mountains.

4. She was wearing a dress <u>of the same blue colour as the sky</u>.
   She was wearing a ______________ dress.

5. For some people, life is a struggle <u>that never ends</u>.
   Life is a ______________ struggle.

6. These chickens are <u>ready for cooking in the oven</u>.
   I always buy ______________ chickens.

 ISBN-978-81-8477-739-0

7. The paintings <u>date from the sixteenth century</u>.
   The castle has a famous collection of ______________ French paintings.

8. The mud on the path was <u>so deep that it came up to our ankles</u>.
   The path was ______________ in mud.

B. In the following sentences, fill in the blanks with compound words that mean the same as the underlined words. The compound words should all be written without hyphens.

1. I bought a new <u>coat to protect me from the rain</u>.
   I bought a new ______________.

2. Parachuting <u>took my breath away</u>.
   Parachuting was a ______________ experience.

3. My grandfather was famous <u>for the songs he wrote and the stories he told</u>.
   I didn't know you were related to a well-known ______________ and ______________.

4. I always got up before <u>the sun rose</u>.
   I always got up before ______________.

C. Underline the adverbial phrases in the following sentences.

1. He was hiding behind the desk.

2. The monks ate their meals in complete silence.

3. The government views the current situation with some alarm.

4. My mother was born in Italy in December 1942.

5. It's so easy, I could do it with my eyes closed.

 ISBN-978-81-8477-739-0

D. Having identified the adverbial phrases in the previous question, state whether they answer the question *when?*, *where?* or *how?*.

1. ______________________________

2. ______________________________

3. ______________________________

4. ______________________________

5. ______________________________

Writing

A. Imagine that you are a journalist. Write an article for your newspaper shortly after the Chernobyl incident took place. Use only the information provided in the passage *Chernobyl*.

____

____

____

____

____

____

____

____

 ISBN-978-81-8477-739-0

B. Research the Fukushima Daiichi nuclear disaster that happened in 2011 in Japan. Write an article for a reference book in the same style as the passage *Chernobyl*.

 ISBN-978-81-8477-739-0

4 Authors and Characters

Comprehension

Read the following story.

Death Play

1 It was a late September morning and the little town of Rockham was just beginning to get ready for another day, when Mrs Sharp hurried into the local shop. Mr and Mrs Wilson, who owned the shop and were busy organising papers for the paper boys and girls to deliver, really did not have time for her right then. Mrs Sharp was the town gossip and they knew that she would talk and talk for ages and stop them from getting on with their work.

2 This morning Mrs Sharp was in a state of ill-concealed excitement. She was the bearer of bad news, but you wouldn't think it to hear her because she seemed to be enjoying every minute of it. Her news was that Old Mr Longhurst had died.

3 Old Mr Longhurst was, in fact, a misnomer because he was only in his mid-fifties. However, he had a son, Jack, and when Jack was in his early twenties and had returned to the town from college, everyone began calling him "Young Mr Longhurst" to distinguish him from his father. As if this were not distinction enough, they started calling his father "Old Mr Longhurst".

4 The Longhursts were the local gentry in Rockham and they had once owned a great deal of land around the town, as well as the manor house. Gradually, the land, and even the manor house had to be sold to pay for inheritance tax and the like. The present Mr Longhurst, at least the one who had just died, lived in what had been the gatehouse to the estate and had only just enough land left to make a reasonable-sized garden.

 ISBN-978-81-8477-739-0

5 People were sad, but not surprised to hear of his death. As a family, the Longhursts were not long-lived and so had suffered more than most from death duties. Of late, little had been seen of Old Mr Longhurst. He was said to be suffering from depression following the recent death of his wife in a riding accident.

6 The day after the announcement of Old Mr Longhurst's death, Mrs Sharp was back in the Wilsons' shop in an even greater state of excitement than before. Old Mr Longhurst had not died of natural causes. He had committed suicide.

7 Now, the people of Rockham usually took what Mrs Sharp said with a pinch of salt. She not only loved gossip, she usually embellished it. However, on this occasion, the Wilsons were inclined to believe her. Mrs Sharp had an excellent source of information at the Longhurst household because her daughter-in-law was a part-time housekeeper there. However terrible the news was, it was probably true – and Old Mr Longhurst had been suffering from depression.

8 Gradually, more details filtered through the town. The deceased had left a note to say that he was taking his own life because he could not face going on living without his adored wife. He apologised to his son for the distress he knew his suicide would cause him. The note had been typed on his computer and left by his bedside, as was the empty bottle which contained the anti-depressant pills which he had taken. An empty whisky bottle stood by the bed.

9 The next thing that the residents of the town heard was that there was going to be a post-mortem. Some were very surprised to hear this, but the more knowledgeable among them, probably the ones who read crime fiction or watched police dramas on television, were aware that post-mortem examinations were routine in cases of sudden death. According to his doctor, Old Mr Longhurst was in excellent physical heath and appeared to have been coming out of his depression before his death.

10 Then came a piece of news that shocked the little town to its very core. It was being suggested that not only had Old Mr Longhurst not died of natural causes, but also that he had been murdered. At first, the more sensible among the townspeople put this suggestion down to rumour-mongering by Mrs Sharp and other gossips in the town. However, the rumour gained credibility when several police officers arrived in the town.

 ISBN-978-81-8477-739-0

11 In no time at all, the rumour, which turned out to be true, became more specific. The police had first become alerted to the fact that something was not quite right when neither the empty pill box, nor the whisky bottle, nor the suicide note contained any fingerprints. It seemed strange to them that someone about to take his own life would go to the trouble to wipe his fingerprints off things. Then the post-mortem did not find any trace of anti-depressant drugs in Mr Longhurst, but it did show significant traces of a particularly virulent weed-killer. A murder investigation had begun!

A. Answer the following questions.

Level 1

1. Use your own words to explain why the Wilsons were not happy to see Mrs Sharp.

____

____

2. What new information did Mrs Sharp share with the Wilsons the day after, and how did she get the news?

____

____

3. What was initially thought to be the reason for the suicide?

____

____

 ISBN-978-81-8477-739-0

4. What was eventually found to be the cause of Mr Longhurst's death?

____

____

Level 2

5. From the description of the Longhursts in paragraph 4, what information can we gather of the family now as compared to the past?

____

____

____

____

____

6. Give two reasons why the post-mortem was called for.

____

____

____

____

____

____

____

 ISBN-978-81-8477-739-0

7. Mr Longhurst's death was greeted with speculation among the townspeople. Using the table below, organise these speculations according to motive or reason and evidence.

Cause	Motive or reason	Evidence
natural death		
committed suicide		
murder		

Level 3

8. Write a word or a short phrase to explain the meaning of the following words as they are used in the passage.

a. ill-concealed ______________________ (paragraph 2)

b. distinguish ______________________ (paragraph 3)

c. embellished ______________________ (paragraph 7)

d. filtered ______________________ (paragraph 8)

e. alerted ______________________ (paragraph 11)

 ISBN-978-81-8477-739-0

Vocabulary

A. This is an exercise on homonyms. Find different meanings of the same words in the following sentences.

1. Dogs bark. Think of a different "bark" and say what sort of plants you associate this type of bark with.

 ___

2. You can keep your money safe in a bank, but where beside water would you find a different sort of bank?

 ___

3. You find pupils in a school, but what sort of animals can you find in schools of a different kind?

 ___

4. Calves are young cows or bulls, but human beings have calves too. What are your calves?

 ___

5. Boots and shoes are footwear, but although cars don't have feet, they have boots as well. What is the boot of a car used for?

 ___

6. A pen is something you write with, but even though sheep can't write, they have pens too. What is a sheep pen?

 ___

 ISBN-978-81-8477-739-0

B. In the following sets of sentences, two of the underlined homonyms rhyme but the third one does not. Circle the sentences which have rhyming homonyms.

1. (a) His mother gave him a terrible <u>row</u> when he came home late.
   (b) He was sitting in the front <u>row</u> of the theatre.
   (c) It isn't hard to <u>row</u> a boat.

2. (a) A single <u>tear</u> ran down her cheek.
   (b) Be careful not to <u>tear</u> the paper.
   (c) Their wedding cake had four tiers, each <u>tier</u> being a different flavour.

3. (a) In the field were a <u>sow</u> and six piglets.
   (b) You should <u>sow</u> the seed earlier if you want a good crop.
   (c) You know how to <u>sew</u> a button on your jacket, don't you?

4. (a) I've been keen on archery ever since I was given a toy <u>bow</u> and arrows as a child.
   (b) The pianist gave a <u>bow</u> at the end of his performance.
   (c) The <u>bow</u> is the front end of a ship.

5. (a) Dogs must be kept on a <u>lead</u> in the park.
   (b) <u>Lead</u> is a soft grey metal.
   (c) The guide <u>led</u> the party of climbers safely off the mountain.

6. (a) There was some sort of fungus growing out of the <u>base</u> of the tree.
   (b) My brother plays the <u>bass</u> guitar.
   (c) A <u>bass</u> is a type of fish.

 ISBN-978-81-8477-739-0

C. Some common English expressions have been picked out in the sentences below. Study the sentences and then write down what you think the idioms mean.

1. She's got a bee in her bonnet about global warming.

2. By the time we got to the beach it was raining cats and dogs.

3. A car like that must have cost a bomb.

4. The service in the restaurant improved by leaps and bounds after the new manager was appointed.

5. You'll need to pull your socks up if you want to pass your exams.

6. I thought it was the wrong decision but I didn't want to rock the boat so I just kept quiet.

 ISBN-978-81-8477-739-0

7. Many other countries are <u>in the same boat</u> as us, with cutbacks in government spending and rising unemployment.

____

____

8. My designs for the new garden just weren't right, so I tore up all my drawings and started again <u>from scratch</u>.

____

____

D. British and American English are very similar, but sometimes they use different words for the same things. Using a dictionary if necessary, write down the British English equivalents of the following words as they are used in American English.

1. sidewalk ____________________
2. airplane ____________________
3. drugstore ____________________
4. hood (of a car) ____________________
5. trunk (of a car) ____________________
6. cookie ____________________
7. candy ____________________
8. aluminum ____________________
9. bill (money) ____________________
10. Mom ____________________

 ISBN-978-81-8477-739-0

Grammar

A. Underline the noun phrases in the following sentences.

1. Without saying another word, he turned around and left the room.
2. Your father is such a kind man.
3. There was a slightly odd young man sitting at a nearby table, studying a rather strange and faded map.
4. Like all the other rooms in the house, my bedroom was both dark and dirty.
5. His sister Mary is a qualified nurse.

B. The words in a noun phrase always come in a particular order. For example, you say "such a friendly old man" and "all the boys", not "a such friendly old man" and "the all boys". Look at the following noun phrases and draw up a table showing the correct relative positions of the words in them.

(Note: use a pencil first – you may change your mind as you analyse the phrases.)

1. a slightly silly child
2. that pretty picture
3. such an amusing story
4. the two very best speakers
5. all the very latest news

 ISBN-978-81-8477-739-0

6. all my best clothes
7. a lovely little old black car
8. the first three really good ideas
9. a quite amazing big yellow bus
10. both those fairly large old brown glass bottles

 ISBN-978-81-8477-739-0

C. On the basis of what you have discovered in exercise B about the structure of noun phrases, re-order the following sets of words to make grammatical sentences.

1. correct entries first prizes substantial the three will win

   ____

2. are boys get going hurt little silly those to two

   ____

3. a book huge it lying old on strange table there was with wooden

   ____

4. a big box cardboard carrying in puppies red she the was

   ____

5. and bike blue come father's my new see

   ____

6. another mine mistake of silly that was

   ____

7. a gifted is musician son such their very Vivek

   ____

8. came extremely holding large mother of out plum shop tarts the their two

   ____

 ISBN-978-81-8477-739-0

D. When quoting what a person has said or written, you must be careful to put only the person's actual words between quotation marks. Compare the sets of sentences below and say which of the following two or three examples correctly indicates the words of the speaker or writer.

1. "I am absolutely amazed to have been selected to receive the prize," said Professor Smith.

    (a) Professor Smith said "he was absolutely amazed" to have been selected to receive the prize.

    (b) Professor Smith said he was "absolutely amazed" to have been selected to receive the prize.

2. "The army will be inside the city walls within a week," the general assured the emperor.

    (a) The general assured the emperor "the army would be inside the city walls within a week".

    (b) The general assured the emperor the army would be "inside the city walls within a week".

    (c) The general assured the emperor the army "would be inside the city walls within a week".

3. "I think visiting the factory would be a little tricky," he said regretfully.

    (a) He said, he thought "visiting the factory would be a little tricky."

    (b) He said, he thought visiting the factory would be "a little tricky".

4. "You have the advantage of me, I think," remarked Margaret as she shook the man's hand.

    (a) As she shook the man's hand, Margaret remarked that he had "the advantage" of her.

 ISBN-978-81-8477-739-0

(b) As she shook the man's hand, Margaret remarked that "he had the advantage of her".

(c) As she shook the man's hand, Margaret remarked that "he had the advantage" of her.

E. American and British English do not only differ in vocabulary, grammar and spelling, they also show a few differences in usage of punctuation. Study the following examples and find two ways in which American and British usage differ.

For example:

American usage: It has been said that "a camel is a racehorse designed by a committee."

British usage: It has been said that 'a camel is a racehorse designed by a committee'.

American usage: The song, which is called "The Heart of Love," is a beautiful ballad.

British usage: The song, which is called 'The Heart of Love', is a beautiful ballad.

Now rewrite the following examples in accordance with British English usage:

1. They call that bone the "funny bone" because its Latin name is the "humerus," which sounds like the English word "humorous".

____

____

 ISBN-978-81-8477-739-0

2. The Government has warned that it is not a question of "whether" an attack will occur, but "when".

3. Many Americans are more concerned about "the American Debt" than "the American Dream".

4. To everyone's surprise, the President ended his speech with "Adios, amigos," which is Spanish for "Goodbye, friends".

Writing

A. A monologue is a text spoken by one person to either himself or to an audience. Write a monologue from the point of view of Mrs Sharp, the town gossip, on the latest rumours of suicide surrounding Mr Longhurst's death. Imagine that she is addressing the Wilsons.

 ISBN-978-81-8477-739-0

 ISBN-978-81-8477-739-0

B. Write a story entitled *The Mystery of the Spiteful Letters* in the style of the passage *Death Play*.

 ISBN-978-81-8477-739-0

5 Myths

Comprehension

Read the following passage.

Theseus Kills the Minotaur

1 Theseus was the son of Aegeus, the king of Athens, although some say that he was really the son of Poseidon, the Greek god of the sea. When Theseus was a baby, his father was concerned for his safety in Athens, and so left the baby and his mother in their country house, about a hundred miles away from Athens. Before leaving for Athens, Aegeus placed a sword beneath a huge boulder. He told his servants that Theseus was to take his place at the court in Athens only when he was strong enough to lift the heavy stone and extract the sword.

2 As he grew up, Theseus went every year to see if he could lift the stone, but each year he failed. Then, when he was about twenty years old, he succeeded in moving the stone and extracting the sword. It was time to join his father and he set off for Athens.

3 When he reached the court, Theseus found his father in a very worried state. Aegeus explained to his son that the cause of his anxiety was a very powerful king called Minos who lived in an island called Crete and who demanded payment from all the Greek cities in order to ensure their safety from him. Aegeus told how Minos would send a ship every year to take away from Athens seven young men and women. They were to be given as sacrifice to a terrible creature called the Minotaur which lived in a great maze, called the Labyrinth, in the palace of King Minos. The Minotaur was half-man and half-bull and lived on human flesh.

4 On hearing that the Cretan ship was due to arrive the very next day, Theseus immediately offered to be one of the seven young men demanded by Minos so that he could kill the Minotaur. His father was horrified at the suggestion. He loved his son dearly and knew that none of the young

 ISBN-978-81-8477-739-0

men or women who had gone to Crete had ever come back. They had been slaughtered by the Minotaur. Theseus, however, insisted, pointing out that it was disgraceful that so many innocent young Athenians had suffered such a cruel fate and that many more would also do so, if Minos was not stopped from making his terrible demands. With great reluctance, the king agreed and Theseus went off in the Cretan ship with the other young people who had been selected as victims.

5 Hearing that the son of the king of Athens was one of the latest set of sacrifices for the Minotaur, Minos ordered Theseus to be brought before him. When Theseus told him that, with the help of the gods, he intended to kill the Minotaur, Minos laughed cruelly. He told Theseus that, even if the Minotaur did not kill him, which was highly unlikely, he would be lost in the Labyrinth.

6 The daughter of King Minos, Ariadne, had overheard his conversation with Theseus. Thinking that this handsome young man must be very brave to defy her father and to try to kill the Minotaur, she resolved to help him.

7 Theseus and the others were taken by their guards to the Labyrinth. Somewhere in the maze of dark, twisting passages lurked the Minotaur, who was waiting to kill and devour them. Just as the guards had turned to leave their prisoners to their fate, Ariadne pushed two objects into Theseus' hands. One was a sword and the other was a ball of wool. Just for a moment, Theseus was puzzled, and then he realised what he must do. Quickly he told one of the other intended victims to hold tight to one strand of the wool, saying that he would take the other end of the strand and make his way through the Labyrinth to find the Minotaur. He would use the wool to help him make his return journey after he had killed the creature. Without the wool, he would surely get lost.

8 Slowly and carefully Theseus moved through the Labyrinth, letting the wool out behind him. It grew darker as he went further into the Labyrinth and he had to grope his way along the twisting passages, still holding the ball of wool tightly as it grew smaller. The labyrinth was silent as well as dark. There was no sign or sound of the Minotaur. Suddenly, the silence was broken by a terrible noise. It was the monster snarling. The terrible beast with the

 ISBN-978-81-8477-739-0

head of a bull charged Theseus and tried to seize him by the throat, but the brave young man fought him off. There was a terrible struggle, during which Theseus thought several times that he was going to die. With the last of his strength, Theseus plunged his trusty sword into the Minotaur's side. The creature gave a terrifying bellow and fell down dead.

A. Answer the following questions.

Level 1

1. What was the test for Theseus' acceptance into the court of Athens?

 ____

 ____

2. What does the passage tell you about the Labyrinth?

 ____

 ____

3. Where did Theseus' unexpected source of help come from and what was it?

 ____

 ____

4. How was the ball of wool useful?

 ____

 ____

 ISBN-978-81-8477-739-0

Level 2

5. How did King Minos show his power over King Aegeus?

____

____

6. Using the table, summarise the reactions of King Aegeus, King Minos and Theseus himself to the latter's mission to kill the Minotaur. Your table should also include the reasons for these reactions.

King Aegeus	King Minos	Theseus

7. Why did Ariadne decide to help Theseus?

____

____

 ISBN-978-81-8477-739-0

8. What evidence from the passage shows that the battle with the Minotaur was a close one for Theseus?

____

____

Level 3

9. Write a word or a short phrase to explain the meaning of the following words as they are used in the passage.

   a. ensure ______________________ (paragraph 3)

   b. disgraceful ______________________ (paragraph 4)

   c. defy ______________________ (paragraph 6)

   d. seize ______________________ (paragraph 8)

   e. plunged ______________________ (paragraph 8)

Vocabulary

A. Using a dictionary, wherever necessary, answer the following questions.

1. What sort of animal is an equine quadruped?

____

2. What sort of remark is a facetious remark?

____

 ISBN-978-81-8477-739-0

3. Would you enjoy watching pyrotechnics?

____

4. Is a metropolis bigger or smaller than a hamlet?

____

5. What would you use a chronometer for?

____

B. Look at the pairs of words in the following examples.

- triangle and tricycle
- trilogy and tripod, where "tri" means three

In the following pair of words, what do the underlined part of the words mean?

1. bilingual, biped

____

2. recurrent, refuel

____

3. quadrangle, quadruple

____

4. forerunner, foresight

____

5. biology, biography

____

 ISBN-978-81-8477-739-0

C. Using a dictionary, wherever necessary, answer the following questions.

1. How many syllables are there in the word "epitome"? Are there the same number of syllables in "catastrophe"?

____

2. What is the plural of "candelabrum"? Is the plural of "conundrum" formed in the same way?

____

3. Is there any difference in the meaning between "demi-", "hemi-" and "semi-"?

____

4. What is the difference between a "flammable" liquid and an "inflammable" liquid?

____

5. What sort of animal do you find in a "pride"?

____

D. Describe the differences in the meanings of the underlined words in the following sentences.

1. The courtiers <u>bowed to</u> the king.
   The courtiers <u>bowed to</u> the king's commands.

____

 ISBN-978-81-8477-739-0

2. The team was disqualified for failing to <u>observe</u> the rules of the game.
"The rules of the game seem to have changed," he <u>observed</u> to his wife.

____

3. I <u>understand</u> that you're leaving tomorrow.
I <u>understand</u> why you're leaving tomorrow.

____

4. The local council <u>maintains</u> the roads very well.
The local council <u>maintains</u> that the roads are in good condition.

____

5. There were some sheep in the <u>field</u>.
Sheep-farming is not really my <u>field</u>.

____

Grammar

A. Fill in the blanks with the correct form of the verb in the following sentences.

1. The luggage ____________ (was / were) piled up in a corner of the room.
2. ____________ (Is / Are) there any news?
3. His wages ____________ (was / were) paid into the bank every week.
4. His views on climate change ____________ (is / are) well known.
5. Cattle ____________ (was / were) grazing on the hillside.
6. Grass ____________ (was / were) growing in the middle of the road.

 ISBN-978-81-8477-739-0

7. The police __________ (was / were) already at the scene of the crime.

8. The audience __________ (was / were) clapping and stamping their feet.

B. Study the pairs of similar sentences below and say whether they are simple, compound or complex sentences. Write **S, Cd** or **Cx** in the brackets.

S = simple sentence **Cd** = compound sentence **Cx** = complex sentence

1. (a) John had a sore arm, so I took him to the doctor. (   )
   (b) John had a sore arm because he fell out of a tree. (   )

2. (a) In 1952, most British households didn't own a television or a car. (   )
   (b) In 1952, most British households didn't own a television and many people didn't have a car. (   )

3. (a) He picked up his coat and hat as he left the house. (   )
   (b) He picked up his coat and hat and went out into the garden. (   )

4. (a) You'll have to go because no one else can. (   )
   (b) You'll have to go if no one else can. (   )

5. (a) When the train stopped, she got out. (   )
   (b) The train had stopped, so she got out. (   )

6. (a) He could write well but he couldn't spell. (   )
   (b) He could write well although he couldn't spell. (   )

7. (a) You'll never persuade him and there's no point in trying. (   )
   (b) You'll never persuade him, so there's no point in trying. (   )

8. (a) That's a very rare stamp and it's worth a lot of money. (   )
   (b) A very rare stamp like that is worth a lot of money. (   )

 ISBN-978-81-8477-739-0

C. Combine the following pairs of simple sentences with a conjunction of your choice (for example, "and", "but", "so", "because", "if", "when") to form either compound or complex sentences. When you have written your answers, decide whether the sentences you have written are compound or complex.

1. I'm not going. John's going.

____

2. It was snowing. Simon waited for a bus.

____

3. We enjoyed the walk. The last steep hill was very hard going.

____

4. She had been away for a year. The locks on all the doors had been changed.

____

5. Mary searched in the garage. Her daughter looked in the garden shed.

____

6. She woke up. There was a terrible noise in the street outside.

____

7. You'll need to buy some milk. There's none in the fridge.

____

 ISBN-978-81-8477-739-0

8. I'm only forty years old. I have seen some incredible changes in the world during my lifetime.

____

D. Complete each of the following sentences in three different ways, with an adverb, with an adverbial phrase and with a subordinate clause.

1. I'll have this job finished ...

____

____

____

2. Joanna felt awful ...

____

____

____

3. He read the paper ...

____

____

____

 ISBN-978-81-8477-739-0

4. The little girl screamed ...

5. Answer all the questions ...

6. Why don't we have a cup of coffee ...

7. Leave your shoes ...

 ISBN-978-81-8477-739-0

8. The children were playing ...

Writing

A. Read the last paragraph of *Theseus Kills the Minotaur*. Rewrite the battle in a vivid and dramatic manner in about 120 words.

 ISBN-978-81-8477-739-0

B. Imagine you are writing for a publication entitled *The Ancient Myths of India*. Retell a myth of your choice.

 ISBN-978-81-8477-739-0

6 Health

Comprehension

Read the following passage.

Lavender

1 More and more people are turning to complementary medicine these days and using it either as an addition to, or as an alternative to, conventional medicine. There are various reasons for this, among them is the fear that modern drugs may be too toxic to the system and that modern surgery is sometimes too drastic.

2 The trend towards complementary medicine has meant a return to many of the old traditional cures. Without a doubt, lavender is one of the most popular of these and, indeed, one of the most versatile, if its advocates are to be believed. It is claimed to be an effective antiseptic, analgesic, antidepressant, sedative and relaxant as well as have the ability to reduce blood pressure and nasal congestion, repel insects and kill intestinal worms.

3 Lavender has been in use for thousands of years, either in the form of essential oil, as it tends to be used now, or in the form of fresh or dried flowers. The plant is native to the Mediterranean region and the best thing is that lavender still grows there. However, the Romans introduced it to northern Europe and it now flourishes all over Europe.

4 The term "lavender" is derived from the Latin word *lavare*, meaning "to wash". Perhaps this was derived from the fact that lavender was used in personal bathing; perhaps it is because it was used in the bathing of wounds. Perhaps both of these forms of cleansing played a part in its origin.

5 Lavender has long played a part in aromatherapy, which has become extremely popular in recent times. When Rene Maurice Gattefosse burnt his hand while conducting a laboratory accident, he used lavender oil on the burnt skin, and was impressed by how quickly the wound healed. This led

 ISBN-978-81-8477-739-0

him to conduct further research into essential oils and their properties. It also led to his coining of the word "aromatherapie", French for aromatherapy. His discovery that lavender aided the healing of burns was confirmed by Dr Jean Valet, a French army surgeon, who used it to treat serious burns, and other injuries, sustained in war. It was later claimed that lavender oil can prevent scarring from burns as well as encourage rapid healing.

6 Lavender has been found to have a healing effect on the mind as well as on the body. It has been found to be particularly useful as an aid to relaxation or as a cure for insomnia. A few drops added to a hot bath before bedtime can help the user both relax and get to sleep more easily. A few drops sprinkled on the pillow can have the same effect.

7 Lavender oil is frequently used in massage, either on its own, or combined with other compatible essential oils. This massage oil is often used for the relief of muscular pain, such as that which occurs in arthritis or rheumatism. Massaged into the temples, lavender oil has been found to relieve many forms of headache.

8 At the very least, lavender is a pleasant sweet-smelling plant. It has long been used to give a pleasant aroma to linen in drawers and chests. Used in this particular way, it is also thought to protect the linen from moths. In the same way, lavender oil, perhaps mixed with other essential oils, such as lemon or bergamot and applied to the skin, is thought to ward off mosquitoes and other insects. Should bites or stings occur, lavender oil is said to take the pain out of the bite or sting and prevent infection.

9 If lavender fulfils at least a few of its alleged cures, it is considerably more wide-ranging in its effectiveness than any drug. Unlike most drugs, it is a very gentle cure without harmful side effects. No wonder it is such a popular remedy.

 ISBN-978-81-8477-739-0

A. Answer the following questions.

Level 1

1. According to the passage, when was lavender first used?

2. In what forms is lavender generally used?

3. Explain the origin of the name "lavender".

4. What incident led to Rene Maurice Gattefosse conducting further research into essential oils?

Level 2

5. What do you understand by the term "complementary medicine"? Why is it gaining popularity?

 ISBN-978-81-8477-739-0

6. Explain how lavender can help someone with difficulty in sleeping.

____

____

7. Write a list of all the benefits and uses of lavender as mentioned in the passage.

____

____

8. Write three adjectives to describe lavender. Do not repeat the words used in the passage.

____

____

Level 3

9. Write a word or short phrase to explain the meaning of the following words as they are used in the passage.

a. versatile ______________________ (paragraph 2)

b. advocates ______________________ (paragraph 2)

c. aromatherapy ______________________ (paragraph 5)

d. compatible ______________________ (paragraph 7)

e. alleged ______________________ (paragraph 9)

 ISBN-978-81-8477-739-0

Vocabulary

A. Choose the matching words in the box with the definitions below. Write in the space provided.

syringe	fracture	crutch	hygiene	tablet

1. A break in a bone. ____________
2. Clean habits and conditions that prevent the spread of disease. ____________
3. A device doctors use to put medicine into your body through a hollow needle. ____________
4. A small solid block of medicine which you put into your mouth and swallow. ____________
5. A long wooden or metal stick with a bar across the top that is used by someone who has an injured foot or leg to support themselves when they are walking. ____________

B. The word "poliomyelitis" consists of three word-forming elements which come to us from Ancient Greek: *polio* meaning "grey", *myel(o)* meaning "marrow" and *-itis* meaning "inflammation". Many other medical terms and names of illnesses are similarly formed from elements derived from Greek. Using a dictionary, find out and write down the meanings of the underlined parts of the following medical terms.

1. <u>neuro</u>logy ____________________________
2. neur<u>osis</u> ____________________________

 ISBN-978-81-8477-739-0

3. neuralgia ______________________

4. gastric ______________________

5. psychology ______________________

6. psychiatry ______________________

7. dermatology ______________________

8. hypodermic ______________________

9. haemorrhage ______________________

10. cardiac ______________________

11. paediatrician ______________________

12. bronchitis ______________________

13. thermometer ______________________

14. pneumonia ______________________

15. arthritis ______________________

What disorders, therefore, do you think "neuritis", "psychosis" and "arthralgia" denote?

____

____

____

____

 ISBN-978-81-8477-739-0

C. Correct the malapropisms in the sentences below. (The incorrect words are underlined.) Rewrite the sentences correctly.

1. There are fire <u>distinguishers</u> in every corridor of the hotel.

2. That's not what happened at all. You must stop jumping to <u>delusions</u>.

3. It's not my fault that the company hasn't made a profit this year, and I won't be made an <u>escape</u> goat!

4. She was admiring the beautiful flower <u>derangements</u> on the tables.

5. Writers whose books don't sell well often say that they are "writing for <u>prosperity</u>".

 ISBN-978-81-8477-739-0

6. The police were called to the scene of the robbery, but the thieves managed to escape in the <u>infusion</u>.

____

____

7. A long walk in the fresh air is the best <u>anecdote</u> to depression.

____

____

8. I would just like to say how much I <u>depreciate</u> the opportunity of addressing you all this evening.

____

____

9. I find it quite <u>incredulous</u> that I have been invited to give this talk.

____

____

10. Whales are related to dolphins and <u>purposes</u>.

____

____

 ISBN-978-81-8477-739-0

D. The sayings and idioms in the following sentences are not in their correct form. (The wrong words are underlined.) Write out the sentences again with the sayings and idioms expressed correctly.

1. Sam and his brother are just like two peas in a <u>pot</u>.

2. She's got a <u>flea</u> in her bonnet about climate change.

3. His plans are just a <u>cardboard</u> copy of what I suggested last week.

4. My husband is like a <u>fool</u> in a china shop when it comes to helping in the kitchen.

 ISBN-978-81-8477-739-0

5. The money we'd get from this job is just chicken <u>feet</u> compared to what we could earn elsewhere.

____

____

6. "There he was," she told the policeman, "lying on the pavement outside my house, as dead as a <u>doorstep</u>!"

____

____

7. It rained <u>carts and logs</u> the whole day long.

____

____

8. The two families had been feuding for years, but they were persuaded to wipe the <u>plate</u> clean and work together for the good of the neighbourhood.

____

____

9. It's a job no one wants to do, but it's time to face our responsibilities and grasp the <u>kettle</u>.

____

____

 ISBN-978-81-8477-739-0

Grammar

A. Write two sentences for each homograph below, one showing its use as a noun and the other showing its use as a verb. And, can you identify the stress patterns for nouns and verbs?

1. export

____

____

2. insult

____

____

3. present

____

____

4. progress

____

____

5. protest

____

____

 ISBN-978-81-8477-739-0

6. rebel

7. record

8. refund

9. torment

10. transport

 ISBN-978-81-8477-739-0

B. Study the sentences below. Decide whether the underlined word is a noun or a verb and based on this, point out which syllable of the word is stressed.

1. Is there a <u>discount</u> if I pay for this with cash?

____

2. There has been a huge <u>increase</u> in traffic along this road recently.

____

3. I <u>suspect</u> he isn't coming after all.

____

4. Do we need a <u>permit</u> to swim here?

____

5. We don't have a screen, so we'll have to <u>project</u> the pictures on to the wall.

____

6. He climbed to the top of the hill from where he could <u>survey</u> the countryside all around him.

____

7. The security guards were called to <u>escort</u> him out of the building.

____

 ISBN-978-81-8477-739-0

8. He was given an award for good <u>conduct</u>.

____

9. You can take the empty bottle back to the shop and they'll <u>refill</u> it.

____

10. There are some really silly <u>misprints</u> in the paper today.

____

C. Fill in the blanks in the sentences below with verbal nouns formed from the underlined verbs.

1. "How do you manage to <u>write</u> poetry?" "Oh, ____________ poems is easy.?"
2. "Have you <u>paid</u> your fare?" "Of course, I have. I wouldn't think of not ____________."
3. I love to <u>ski</u>. ____________ is my favourite hobby.
4. I really must <u>get</u> fit. ____________ fit is a top priority now.
5. Another thing I need to do is <u>lose</u> weight. But ____________ weight is really hard.
6. You're not allowed to <u>smoke</u> here. The notice over there says "No ____________".
7. Samira just picked up her bag and <u>left</u> the room. Her ____________ so abruptly quite surprised us.

 ISBN-978-81-8477-739-0

8. When he <u>broke</u> the vase, John apologised profusely for ______ it.

9. I <u>sold</u> three paintings last week. I make a lot of money from ______ my work.

10. How many cups of coffee have you <u>drunk</u> today? ______ that much coffee is not good for you, you know.

D. Words ending in "-ing" play a number of roles in English sentences. They may be verbs (present participles), as in "I am <u>going</u> home". They may be adjectives, as in "a very <u>boring</u> programme". They may be nouns, as in "a famous <u>painting</u> by Picasso". And they may be verbal nouns (gerunds), as in "<u>Hitting</u> people is not allowed" or "You could help by <u>washing</u> the dishes". Now, look at the "-ing" words in the following sentences and say whether they are participles, adjectives, nouns or verbal nouns.

Write **P**, **A**, **N** or **Vn** in the brackets.

P = participle   **A** = adjective
N = noun   **Vn** = verbal noun

1. What are you reading now? ( )
   The children are all very good at reading. ( )
2. Painting is a very relaxing hobby. ( )
   He owns several paintings by Picasso. ( )
3. Have you any useful advice on growing tomatoes? ( )
   We're not growing tomatoes this year. ( )

 ISBN-978-81-8477-739-0

4. Is something worrying you? ( )
The worrying thing is, we don't know what's wrong. ( )
Worrying about your health can make you feel even worse. ( )

5. The children are all learning to read and write. ( )
By learning to read, you improve your chances of getting a good job. ( )

6. Everyone was laughing. ( )
We just couldn't help laughing. ( )

7. He had been swimming for about half an hour. ( )
After swimming for so long, he felt very tired. ( )

8. I've got a very important meeting this afternoon. ( )
Meeting people is very important. ( )

9. I wish you two would stop arguing. ( )
Arguing with her was a complete waste of time. ( )

10. I find their children very irritating. ( )
They were irritating me all evening. ( )
They seem to enjoy irritating people. ( )

E. Some compound nouns are formed with verbal nouns as the first element (for example, a "walking stick", a "cooking pot"). Compounds formed with verbal nouns usually denote something that has a particular purpose (a "cooking pot", for example, is a pot you use for cooking). Fill in the blanks in the following sentences with compounds formed with verbal nouns.

1. If your clothes are very dirty, you should wash them in the ______________________.

 ISBN-978-81-8477-739-0

2. A long thin pole that is used to catch fish is a
_______________________.

3. The high board from which people jump into a swimming pool is called a _______________________.

4. A very fast car that is used in sporting competitions is a
_______________________.

5. A device that tells you how heavy you are is a _______________.

6. A wide shallow pan that you cook food in is a _______________.

7. The wheel in a car that you turn to make the car go left or right is the
_______________________.

8. If you have difficulty sleeping, you may take a _______________ to help you sleep.

9. The room in a house in which people eat their meals is called the
_______________________.

10. When you visit the dentist, you may have to sit in the
_______________________ until the dentist is ready to see you.

 ISBN-978-81-8477-739-0

Writing

A. What are your views about the usefulness of lavender as a complementary medicine? You may need to do some research in addition to using the information from the passage *Lavender*.

 ISBN-978-81-8477-739-0

B. Write about another complementary or traditional medicine commonly used in India.

 ISBN-978-81-8477-739-0